Let's Read About...
Christopher Columbus

To Gina,
a wonderful editor and friend
—K. W.

To Jon on his exploits
of the right side of the brain
—C.V.W. and Y.-H. H.

The editors would like to thank
Keith Pickering for his expertise.

ISBN: 0-439-29546-7

Text copyright © 2001 by Kimberly Weinberger.
Illustrations copyright © 2001 by Cornelius Van Wright and Ying-Hwa Hu.

Library of Congress Cataloging-in-Publication Data

Weinberger, Kimberly.
　　Let's read about — Christopher Columbus / by Kimberly Weinberger ; illustrated by Cornelius Van Wright and Ying-Hwa Hu.
　　　　p.　　cm. — (Scholastic first biographies)
　　Summary: A simple biography of the Italian explorer who became the first European to discover the West Indies islands in three historic voyages sponsored by Spain's monarchy.
　　　　ISBN 0-439-29546-7
　　　　1. Columbus, Christopher — Juvenile literature. 2. Explorers — America — Biography — Juvenile literature. 3. Explorers — Spain — Biography — Juvenile literature. 4. America — Discovery and exploration — Spanish — Juvenile literature. [1. Columbus, Christopher. 2. Explorers. 3. America — Discovery and exploration — Spanish.] I. Van Wright, Cornelius, ill. II. Hu, Ying-Hwa, ill. III. Series.
　　E111 .W432 2001
　　970.01'5'092—dc21　　　　　　　　　　　　　　　　　　2001034479
　　[B]

10　9　8　7　6　5　4　3　2　1　　　　　　　　　　　　01　02　03　04　05　06

Printed in the U.S.A.
First printing, October 2001

Let's Read About...
Christopher Columbus

Scholastic
First Biographies

by Kimberly Weinberger

Illustrated by Cornelius Van Wright
and Ying-Hwa Hu

SCHOLASTIC INC. Cartwheel
·B·O·O·K·S·®

New York   Toronto   London   Auckland   Sydney
Mexico City   New Delhi   Hong Kong   Buenos Aires

Christopher Columbus was born in Italy more than 500 years ago.

Columbus lived near the sea in a city
called Genoa.
He loved to watch ships come and go.
He wished he could sail away
on them!

As a child, Columbus worked
with his father making cloth.
But the young boy dreamed only
of a life at sea.

Columbus's dream came
true when he turned 14
years old.
He got a job as a helper
on a ship.
Soon he was a real sailor.

Columbus loved his new life.
He took many trips.
He saw many cities.
He heard people speak of rich,
faraway places.
And what was the most
wonderful place of all?
The Indies!

The Indies was a land filled with
gold and spices.
But getting there was very hard.
The mountains and deserts in
between were dangerous.
So Columbus had a better idea!

Everyone knew the Indies lay across the land, far to the east.
But only Columbus thought he could get there by sailing *west*.

He would do what no one thought
was possible.
He would cross the Great Western
Ocean!

King Ferdinand and Queen Isabella
of Spain agreed to pay for Columbus's trip.
People in other countries thought
Columbus was crazy!
They were sure he would never make it all
the way across the ocean.
Columbus promised to bring riches back
to Spain.
He set sail on August 3, 1492.

Columbus took three ships: the *Niña,* the *Pinta,* and the *Santa Maria.* He brought about 100 men with him. They sailed across the lonely ocean for weeks and weeks.

Columbus's men were scared and tired.
Would they ever reach land?
Yes!
On October 12, 1492, they saw it—
a bright, green island.
They had reached the Indies at last!

Or had they?

Friendly people welcomed Columbus to their land.
These natives had never seen people with skin so white.

They had never seen men wear
so much clothing.
They thought Columbus must
have fallen from the sky!

Columbus called the natives Indians.
He gave them small bells that jingled.
They gave him fruit, thread,
and parrots.
But where is the gold?
Columbus wondered.

Columbus placed the flag of Spain
on the island.
He thought the land now belonged
to that country.

He did not ask the natives if this was okay.

Today we know that Columbus made a mistake.
He did not find a path to the Indies.
He found the New World.

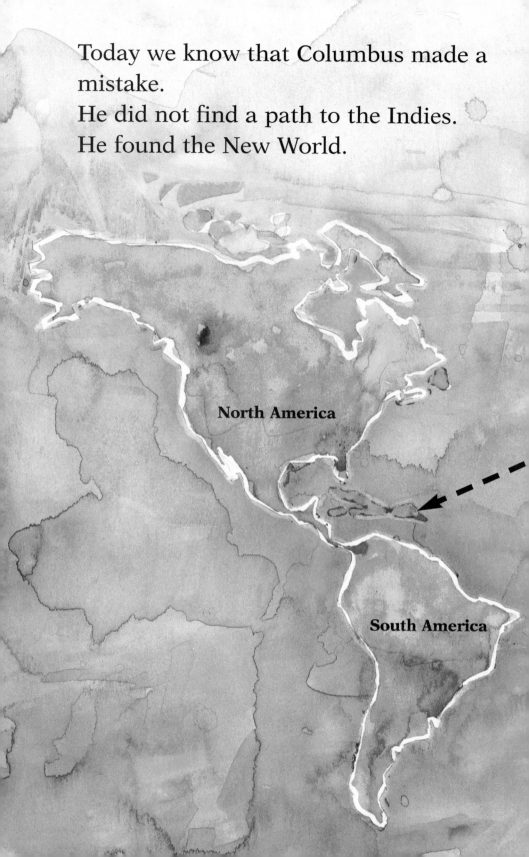

North America

South America

Of course, it was not new to the people
who lived there!
We now call these lands North America
and South America.

Columbus never did find all of the gold he wanted.
But we remember him today as a brave sailor.
And we honor him for his mistake!